The Necklace
The Pearls

Guy de Maupassant

The Necklace

Isak Dinesen

The Pearls

The Necklace
translated from the French by
Jonathan Sturges

Pushkin Press
London

The Necklace first published in French in 1891

The Pearls © 1942 by Random House Inc. Copyright © renewed
1970 by Johan Philip Thomas Ingerslev. This edition is published
with the permission of the Rungstedlund Foundation and is based
on the text of the revised edition published by Putnam 1958. Taken
from the Penguin Twentieth Century Classics edition of *Winter's
Tales*, first published by Penguin Books Ltd in 1983.

This edition first published in 1999 by
Pushkin Press
22 Park Walk
London SW10 0AQ

British Library Cataloguing in Publication Data:
A catalogue record for this book is available
from the British Library

ISBN 1 901285 26 X

Set in 11 on 14 Baskerville
and printed in France by Expressions, Paris
on Rives Classic Laid

Cover illustration: *Angel*
Jason Martin

The Necklace

THE NECKLACE

S HE WAS ONE of those pretty and charming young
girls who sometimes are born, as if by a slip of
fate, into a family of clerks. She had no dowry, no
expectations, no way of being known, understood,
loved, and wedded by any rich and distinguished
man; so she let herself be married to a little clerk of
the Ministry of Public Instruction.

She dressed plainly because she could not dress
well, but she was as unhappy as if she had really fall-
en from a higher station; since with women there is
neither caste nor rank, for beauty, grace and charm
take the place of birth and breeding. Natural inge-
nuity, instinct for what is elegant, a supple mind are
their sole hierarchy, and often make of women of
the people the equals of the very greatest ladies.

Mathilde suffered ceaselessly, feeling herself born
to enjoy all delicacies and all luxuries. She was distressed at the poverty of her dwelling, at the bare-
ness of the walls, at the shabby chairs, the ugliness of
the curtains. All those things, of which another
woman of her rank would never even have been
conscious, tortured her and made her angry. The

sight of the little Breton peasant who did her humble housework aroused in her despairing regrets and bewildering dreams. She thought of silent antechambers hung with Oriental tapestries, illuminated by tall bronze candelabra, and of two great footmen in knee breeches who sleep in the big armchairs, made drowsy by the oppressive heat of the stove. She thought of long reception halls hung with ancient silk, of the dainty cabinets containing priceless curiosities and of little coquettish perfumed reception rooms made for chatting at five o'clock with intimate friends, with men famous and sought after, whom all women envy and whose attention they all desire.

When she sat down to dinner, before the round table covered with a tablecloth in use three days, opposite her husband, who uncovered the soup tureen and declared with a delighted air, "Ah, the good soup! I don't know anything better than that," she thought of dainty dinners, of shining silverware, of tapestry that peopled the walls with ancient personages and with strange birds lying in the midst of a fair forest; and she thought of delicious dishes served on marvellous plates and of the whispered gallantries to which you listen with a sphinx-like smile while you are eating the wings of a quail.

She had no gowns, no jewels, nothing. And she loved nothing but that. She felt made for that. She would have liked so much to please, to be envied, to be charming, to be sought after.

She had a friend, a former schoolmate at the convent, who was rich, and whom she did not like to go to see any more because she felt so sad when she came home. But one evening her husband came home with a triumphant air and holding a large envelope in his hand.

"There," said he, "there is something for you." She tore the paper quickly and drew out a printed card which bore these words:

"The Minister of Public Instruction and Madame Georges Ramponneau request the honour of M. and Madame Loisel's company at the palace of the Ministry on Monday evening, January 18th."

Instead of being delighted, as her husband had hoped, she threw the invitation on the table crossly, muttering:

"What do you wish me to do with that?"

"Why, my dear, I thought you would be glad. You never go out, and this is such a fine opportunity. I had great trouble getting it. Everyone wants to go; it is very select, and they are not giving many invitations to clerks. The whole official world will be there."

She looked at him with an irritated glance and said impatiently:

"And what do you wish me to put on my back?"

"He had not thought of that." He stammered:

"Why, the gown you go to the theatre in. It looks very well to me."

Her husband stopped, distracted, seeing that his wife was weeping. Two great tears ran slowly from the corners of her eyes towards the corners of her mouth.

"What's the matter? What's the matter?" he asked.

By a violent effort she conquered her grief and replied in a calm voice, while she wiped away her tears:

"Nothing. Only I have no gown, and, therefore, I can't go to this ball. Give your card to some colleague whose wife is better equipped than I am."

He was in despair. He resumed:

"Come, let us see, Mathilde. How much would it cost, a suitable gown, which you could use on other occasions—something very simple?"

She reflected several seconds, making her calculations and wondering also what sum she could ask without drawing on herself an immediate refusal and a frightened exclamation from the economical clerk.

Finally she replied hesitatingly:

"I don't know exactly, but I think I could manage it with four hundred francs."

He grew a little pale, because he was laying aside just that amount to buy a gun and treat himself to a little shooting next summer on the plain of Nanterre, with several friends who went to shoot larks there of a Sunday.

But he said:

"Very well. I will give you four hundred francs. And try to have a pretty gown."

The day of the ball drew near and Madame Loisel seemed sad, uneasy, anxious. Her frock was ready, however. Her husband said to her one evening:

"What is the matter? Come, you have seemed very strange these last three days."

And she answered:

"It annoys me not to have a single piece of jewellery, not a single ornament, nothing to put on. I shall look poverty-stricken. I would almost rather not go at all."

"You might wear natural flowers," said her husband. "They're quite fashionable at this time of year. For ten francs you can get two or three magnificent roses."

She was not convinced.

"No; there's nothing more humiliating than to look poor among other women who are rich."

"How stupid you are!" her husband cried. "Go and look up your friend, Madame Forestier, and ask her to lend you some jewels. You're intimate enough with her to do that."

She uttered a cry of joy:

"True! I never thought of it."

The next day she went to her friend and told her of her distress.

Madame Forestier went to a wardrobe with a mirror, took out a large jewel box, brought it back, opened it and said to Madame Loisel:

"Choose, my dear."

She saw first some bracelets, then a pearl necklace, then a Venetian gold cross set with precious stones, of admirable workmanship. She tried on the ornaments before the mirror, hesitated and could not make up her mind to part with them, to give them back. She kept asking:

"Haven't you any more?"

"Why, yes. Look further; I don't know what you like."

Suddenly she discovered, in a black satin box, a superb diamond necklace, and her heart throbbed with an immoderate desire. Her hands trembled as she took it. She fastened it round her throat, and was lost in ecstasy at her reflection in the mirror.

Then she asked, hesitating, filled with anxious doubt:

"Will you lend me this, only this?"

"Why, yes, certainly."

She threw her arms round her friend's neck, kissed her passionately, and then fled with her treasure.

The night of the ball arrived. Madame Loisel was a great success. She was prettier than any other woman present, elegant, graceful, smiling and filled with joy. All the men looked at her, asked her name, sought to be introduced. All the attachés of the Cabinet wished to waltz with her. She was remarked on by the minister himself.

She danced with rapture, with passion, intoxicated by pleasure, forgetting all in the triumph of her beauty, in the glory of her success, in a sort of cloud of happiness composed of all this homage and admiration, and of that sense of triumph which is so sweet to a woman's heart.

She left the ball at about four o'clock in the morning. Her husband had been sleeping since midnight in a little deserted anteroom with three other gentlemen whose wives were enjoying the ball.

He threw over her shoulders the wrap he had brought, the modest, commonplace wrap of common life, the poverty of which contrasted with the elegance of the ball dress. She felt this and wished to escape so as not to be remarked on by the other woman, who were enveloping themselves in costly furs.

Loisel held her back, saying: "Wait a bit. You will catch cold outside. I will call a cab."

But she did not listen to him and rapidly descended the stairs. When they reached the street they could not find a carriage and began to look for one, shouting after the cabmen passing at a distance.

They went towards the Seine in despair, shivering with cold. At last they found on the quay one of those ancient night cabs which, as though they were ashamed to show their shabbiness during the day, are never seen round Paris until after dark.

It took them to their dwelling on the Rue des Martyrs, and sadly they mounted the stairs to their flat. All was ended for her. As for him, he reflected that he must be at the Ministry at ten o'clock that morning.

She removed her wrap before the glass so as to see herself once more in all her glory. But suddenly she uttered a cry. She no longer had the necklace round her neck.

"What is the matter with you?" demanded her husband, already half undressed.

She turned distractedly towards him.

"I have—I have—I've lost Madame Forestier's necklace," she cried.

He stood up, bewildered.

"What!—how? That's impossible!"

They looked among the folds of her skirt, of her cloak, in her pockets, everywhere, but did not find it.

"You're sure you had it on when you left the hall?" he asked.

"Yes, I felt it in the vestibule of the minister's house."

"But if you had lost it in the street we should have heard it fall. It must be in the cab."

"Yes, probably. Did you take his number?"

"No. And you—didn't you notice it?"

"No."

They looked, thunderstruck, at each other. At last Loisel put on his clothes.

"I shall go back on foot," said he, "over the whole route, to see whether I can find it."

He went out. She sat waiting on a chair in her ball dress, without strength to go to bed, overwhelmed, without any fire, without a thought.

Her husband returned at about seven o'clock. He had found nothing.

He went to police headquarters, to the newspaper offices to offer a reward; he went to the cab companies—everywhere, in fact, whither he was urged by the least spark of hope.

She waited all day, in the same condition of mad fear before this terrible calamity.

Loisel returned at night with a hollow, pale face. He had discovered nothing.

"You must write to your friend," said he, "that you have broken the clasp of her necklace and that you are having it mended. That will give us time to turn round."

She wrote at his dictation.

At the end of a week they had lost all hope. Loisel, who had aged five years, declared:

"We must consider how to replace that ornament."

The next day they took the box that had contained it and went to the jeweller whose name was found within. He consulted his books.

"It was not I, madame, who sold that necklace; I must simply have furnished the case."

Then they went from jeweller to jeweller, searching for a necklace like the other, trying to recall it, both sick with chagrin and grief.

They found, in a shop at the Palais Royal, a string of diamonds that seemed to them exactly like the one they had lost. It was worth forty thousand francs. They could have it for thirty-six.

So they begged the jeweller not to sell it for three days yet. And they made a bargain that he should buy it back for thirty-four thousand francs, in case they should find the lost necklace before the end of February.

Loisel possessed eighteen thousand francs which his father had left him. He would borrow the rest.

He did borrow, asking a thousand francs of one, five hundred of another, five *louis* here, three *louis* there. He gave notes, took up ruinous obligations, dealt with usurers and all that race of moneylenders. He compromised all the rest of his life, risked signing a note without even knowing whether he could meet it; and, frightened by the trouble yet to come, by the black misery that was about to fall upon him, by the prospect of all the physical privations and moral tortures that he was to suffer, he went to get the new necklace, laying upon the jeweller's counter thirty-six thousand francs.

When Madame Loisel took back the necklace Madame Forestier said to her with a chilly manner:

"You should have returned it sooner; I might have needed it."

She did not open the case, as her friend had so much feared. If she had detected the substitution, what would she have thought, what would she have said? Would she not have taken Madame Loisel for a thief? Thereafter Madame Loisel knew the horrible existence of the needy. She bore her part, however, with sudden heroism. That dreadful debt must be paid; she would pay it. They dismissed their servant; they changed their lodgings; they rented a garret under the roof.

She came to know what heavy housework meant and the odious cares of the kitchen. She washed the dishes, using her dainty fingers and rosy nails on greasy pots and pans. She washed the soiled linen, the shirts and the dishcloths, which she dried upon a line; she took the slops down to the street every morning and carried up the water, stopping for breath at every landing. And dressed like a woman of the people, she went to the fruiterer, the grocer, the butcher, a basket on her arm, bargaining, meeting with impertinence, defending her miserable money, *sou* by *sou*.

Every month they had to meet some notes, renew others, obtain more time.

Her husband worked in the evenings, making up a tradesman's accounts, and late at night he often copied manuscripts for five *sous* a page.

This life lasted ten years.

At the end of ten years they had paid everything, everything with the rates of usury and the accumulations of compound interest.

Madame Loisel looked old now. She had become the woman of impoverished households strong and hard and rough. With brown hair, skirts askew and red hands, she talked aloud while washing the floor with great swishes of water. But sometimes, when her husband was at the office, she sat down near the window and thought of that gay evening of long ago, of that ball where she had looked so beautiful and been so much admired.

What would have happened if she had not lost that necklace? Who knows? who knows? How strange and surprising is life! How small a thing is needed to make or ruin us!

But one Sunday, having gone for a walk in the Champs Elysées to refresh herself after the labours of the week, she suddenly saw a woman who was leading a child. It was Madame Forestier, still young, still beautiful, still charming.

Madame Loisel felt moved. Should she speak to her? Yes, certainly. And now that she had paid, she would tell her all about it. Why not?

She approached her.

"Good day, Jeanne."

The other, astonished to be familiarly addressed by this plain housewife, did not recognize her at all and stammered: "But—madame!—I do not know—You must be mistaken."

"No. I am Madame Loisel."

Her friend uttered a cry.

"Oh, my poor Mathilde! How you are changed!"

"Yes, I have had a very hard life—since I last saw you, and great poverty—and that because of you!"

"Of me! How so?"

"Do you remember that diamond necklace you lent me to wear at the Ministerial ball?"

"Yes. Well?"

"Well, I lost it." "What do you mean? You brought it back."

"I brought you back another exactly like it. And it has taken us ten years to pay for it. You can understand that it was not easy for us, for us who had nothing. At last it is ended, and I am very glad."

Madame Forestier had stopped.

"You say that you bought a necklace of diamonds to replace mine?"

"Yes. You never noticed it, then! They were very similar."

And she smiled with a joy that was at once proud and ingenuous.

Madame Forestier, deeply moved, took her hands.

"Oh, my poor Mathilde! Why, my necklace was paste! It was worth at most only five hundred francs!"

The Pearls

THE PEARLS

ABOUT EIGHTY YEARS AGO, a young officer in the guards, the younger son of an old country family, married in Copenhagen the daughter of a rich wool merchant, whose father had been a pedlar and had come to town from Jutland. In those days, such a marriage was an unusual thing, there was much talk of it, and a song was made about it, and sung in the streets.

The bride was twenty years old, and a beauty,—a big girl with black hair and a high colour, and a distinction about her as if she were made from whole timber. She had two old unmarried aunts, sisters of her grandfather the pedlar, whom the growing fortune of the family had stopped short in a career of hard work and thrift, and made to sit in state in a parlour. When the elder of them first heard rumours of her niece's engagement, she went and paid her a visit, and in the course of their conversation told her a story.

"When I was a child, my dear," she said, "young Baron Rosenkrantz became engaged to a wealthy goldsmith's daughter, have you heard such a thing? Your great-grandmother knew her. The bridegroom had a twin sister, who was a lady at Court, she drove to the goldsmith's house to see the bride. When she had left again, the girl said to her lover: 'Your sister laughed at my frock, and also, when she spoke French, I could not answer. She has a hard heart, I saw that. If we are to be happy you must never see her again, I could not bear it.' The young man, to comfort her, promised that he would never see his sister again. Soon afterwards, on a Sunday, he took the girl to dine with his mother. As he drove her home she said to him: 'Your mother had tears in her eyes, when she looked at me, she has hoped for another wife for you. If you love me, you must break with your mother.' Again the enamoured young man promised to do as she wished, although it cost him much, for his mother was a widow, and he was her only son. The same week he sent his valet with a bouquet to his bride. Next day, she said to him: 'I cannot stand the mien your valet has when he looks at me. You must send him away at the first of the month.' 'Mademoiselle,' said Baron Rosenkrantz, 'I cannot have a wife who lets herself be affected by my valet's mien; here is your ring; farewell forever.' "

While the old woman spoke she kept her little glittering eyes upon her niece's face. She had an energetic nature, and had long ago made up her mind to live for others, and she had established herself as the conscience of the family. But in reality she was, with no hopes or fears of her own, a vigorous, old, moral parasite on the whole clan and particularly on the younger members of it. Jensine, the bride, was a full-blooded young person and a gratifying object to a parasite, moreover the young and the old maid had many qualities in common. Now the girl went on pouring out coffee with a quiet face, but behind it she was furious, and said to herself: "Aunt Maren shall be paid back for this." All the same, as was often the case, the aunt's admonitions went deep into her, and she pondered them in her heart.

After the wedding, in the Cathedral of Copenhagen, on a fine June day, the newly married couple went away to Norway for their wedding trip; they sailed as far north as Hardanger. At that time, a journey to Norway was a romantic undertaking, and Jensine's friends asked her why they did not go to Paris, but she herself was pleased to start her married life in the wilderness, and to be alone with her husband. She did not, she thought, want or need any further impressions or experiences. And in her heart she added: "God help me."

The gossips of Copenhagen would have it that the bridegroom had married for money, and the bride for a name, but they were all wrong. The match was a love-affair, and the honeymoon, technically, an idyll. Jensine would never have married a man whom she did not love, she held the God of love in great respect, and had already for some years sent a little daily prayer to him: "Why dost thou tarry?" But now she reflected that he had perhaps granted her her prayer with a vengeance, and that her books had given her but little information as to the real nature of love.

The scenery of Norway, amongst which she made her first experience of the passion, contributed to the overpowering impression of it. The country was at its loveliest, the sky was blue, the bird cherry flowered everywhere and filled the air with sweet and bitter fragrance, and the nights were so light that you could see to read at midnight. Jensine, in a crinoline and with an alpenstock, climbed many steep paths on her husband's arm,—or alone, for she was strong and light-footed,—she stood upon the summits, her clothes blown about her, and wondered and wondered. She had lived in Denmark, and for a year in a pension in Lubeck, and her idea of the earth was that it must spread out horizontally, flat or undulating, before her feet. But in these mountains, everything seemed strangely to stand up vertically, like some great animal that rises on its hindlegs,—and you know not whether it is to play, or to crush you. She was so high up as she had never been, and the air went to her head like wine. Also wherever she looked there was running water, rushing from the sky-high mountains into the lakes, in silvery rivulets or in roaring falls, rainbow-adorned,—it was as if Nature itself was weeping, or laughing, aloud.

At first all this was so new to her that she felt her old ideas of the world blown about in all directions, like her skirts and her shawl. But soon the impressions converged into a sensation of the deepest alarm, a panic such as she had never experienced.

She had been brought up in an atmosphere of prudence and foresight. Her father was an honest tradesman, afraid both to lose his own money, and to let down his customers; sometimes this double risk had thrown him into melancholia. Her mother had been a God-fearing young woman, a member of a pietistic sect, her two old aunts were persons of strict moral principle, with an eye to the opinions of

the world. At home Jensine had at times believed
herself a daring spirit, and had longed for adven-
ture. But in this wildly romantic landscape, and
taken by surprise and overwhelmed by wild,
unknown, formidable forces within her own heart,
she looked round for support, and where was she to
find it? Her young husband, who had brought her
there, and with whom she was all alone, could not
help her. He was, on the contrary, the cause of the
turbulence in her, and he was also, in her eyes, pre-
eminently exposed to the dangers of the outward
world. For very soon after her marriage, Jensine
realised—as she had perhaps dimly known from
their first meeting,—that he was a human being
entirely devoid, and incapable of fear.

She had read in books of heroes, and had admired
them with all her heart. But Alexander was not like
the heroes of her books. He was not braving or con-
quering the dangers of this world, but he was
unaware of their existence. To him, the mountains
were a playground, and all the phenomena of life,
love itself included, were his playmates within it.

"In a hundred years, my darling," he said to her,
"it will all be one."

She could not imagine how he had managed to

live till now, but then she knew that his life had been in every way different from hers. Now she felt, with horror, that here she was, within a world of undreamt-of heights and depths, delivered into the hands of a person totally ignorant of the law of gravity. Under the circumstances, her feelings for him intensified into both a deep moral indignation, as if he had deliberately betrayed her, and into an extreme tenderness, such as she would have felt towards an exposed, helpless child. These two passions were the strongest of which her nature was capable; they took speed with her, and developed into a possession. She recalled the fairy tale of the boy who is sent out into the world to learn to be afraid, and it seemed to her that for her own sake and his, in self defence, as well as in order to protect and save him, she must teach her husband to fear.

He knew nothing of what went on in her. He was in love with her, and he admired and respected her. She was innocent and pure, she sprang from a stock of people capable of making a fortune by their wits, she could speak French and German, and knew history and geography. For all these qualities he had a religious reverence. He was prepared for surprises in her, for their acquaintance was but slight, and they had not been alone together in a room more than three or four times before their wedding. Besides he did not pretend to understand women, but held their incalculableness to be part of their grace. The moods and caprices of his young wife all confirmed in him the assurance, with which she had inspired him at their first meeting, that she was what he needed in life. But he wanted to make her his friend, and reflected that he had never had a real friend in his life.

He did not talk to her of his love affairs of the past, indeed he could not have spoken of them to her if he had wanted to, but in other ways he told her as much as he could remember of himself and his life. One day he recounted how he had gambled in Baden-Baden, risked his last *mark*, and then won. He did not know that she thought, by his side: "He is really a thief, or if not that, a receiver of stolen goods, and no better than a thief."

At other times he made fun of the debts he had had, and the trouble he had had to take to avoid meeting his tailor. This talk sounded really uncanny to Jensine's ears. For to her, debts were an abomination, and that he should have lived on in the midst of them without anxiety, trusting to fortune to pay

up for him, seemed against nature. Still, she reflected, she herself, the rich girl he had married, had
come along in time, as the willing tool of fortune, to
justify his trust in the eyes of his tailor himself.

He told her of a duel that he had fought with a
German officer, and showed her a scar from it.

As, at the end of it all, he took her in his arms, on
the high hilltops, for all the skies to see them; in her
heart she cried: "If it be possible, let this cup pass
from me."

When Jensine set out to teach her husband to fear,
she had the tale of Aunt Maren in her mind, and she
made the vow that she would never cry quarter, but
that this must be his part. As the relation between
herself and him was to her the central factor of existence, it was natural that she should first try to scare
him with the possibility of losing her, herself. She
was an unsophisticated girl and resorted to simple
measures.

From now on she became more reckless than he
in their climbs. She would stand on the edge of a
precipice, leaning on her parasol, and ask him how
deep it was to the bottom. She balanced across nar-
row, brittle bridges, high above foaming streams,
and chattered to him the while, she went out rowing

in a small boat, on the lake, in a thunderstorm. At nights she dreamed about the perils of the days, and woke up with a shriek, so that he took her in his arms to comfort her. But her daring did her no good. Her husband was surprised and enchanted at the change of the demure maiden into a Walkyrie; he put it down to the influence of married life, and felt not a little proud. She herself, in the end, wondered whether she was not driven on in her exploits by his pride and praise, as much as by her resolution to conquer him; then she was angry with herself, and with all women, and she pitied him, and all men.

Sometimes Alexander would go out fishing. These were welcome opportunities to Jensine to be alone and collect her thoughts. So the young bride would wander about alone, in a tartan frock, a small figure in the hills. Once or twice, in these walks, she thought of her father, and the memory of his anxious concern for her, brought tears to her eyes. But she sent him away again; she must be left alone to settle matters of which he could know nothing.

One day, when she sat and rested on a stone, a group of children, who were herding goats, approached and stared at her. She called them up, and gave them sweets from her reticule. Jensine had adored her dolls, and as much as a modest girl of the period dared, she had longed for children of her own. Now she thought with sudden dismay: "I shall never have children! As long as I must strain myself against him in this way, we will never have a child." The idea distressed her so deeply that she got up and walked away.

On another of her lonely walks she came to think of a young man in her father's office, who had loved her. His name was Peter Skov, he was a brilliant young man of business, and she had known him all her life. She now recalled how, when she had had the measles, he had sat and read to her every day, and how he had accompanied her when she went out skating, and had been distressed lest she should catch cold, or fall, or go through the ice. From where she stood, she could see her husband's small figure in the distance. "Yes," she thought, "this is the best thing I can do. When I get back to Copenhagen, then by my honour, which is still my own," although she had doubts about this point, "Peter Skov shall be my lover."

On their wedding day Alexander had given his bride a string of pearls. It had belonged to his Grandmother, who had come from Germany, and

who was a beauty and a *bel esprit*; she had left it to
him to give to his future wife. Alexander had talked
much to her of his Grandmother; he said he first fell
in love with her, because she was a little like his
Grandmamma: he asked her to wear the pearls
always.

Jensine had never had a string of pearls before,
and she was proud of them.

Lately, when she had so often been in need of support, she had got into the habit of twisting the string,
and pulling it with her lips.

"If you go on doing that," Alexander said one day,
"you will break the string."

She looked at him. It was the first time that she
had known him to foresee disaster. "He loved his
Grandmother," she thought, "or is it that you must
be dead to carry weight with this man?"

Since then she often thought of the old woman. She,
too, had come from her own *milieu* and had been a
stranger in her husband's family and circle of friends.
She had at last managed to get this string of pearls
from Alexander's Grandfather, and it was remembered of her. Were the pearls, she wondered, a token
of victory, or of submission? Jensine came to look
upon Grandmamma as her best friend in the family,

she would have liked to pay her a grand-daughterly visit, and to consult her on her own troubles.

The honeymoon was nearing its end, and that strange warfare, the existence of which was known to one of the belligerents only, had come to no decision. Both the young people were sad to go away. Only now, did Jensine fully realise the beauty of the landscape round her, for after all, in the end she had made it her ally. Up here, she reflected, the dangers of the world were obvious,—always in sight. In Copenhagen, life looked secure, but might prove to be even more redoubtable. She thought of her pretty house, waiting for her there, with lace curtains, chandeliers and linen cupboards; she could not tell what life within it would be like.

The day before they were to sail they were staying in a small village, from where it was six hours' drive in a carriage down to the landing-stage of the coast steamer. They had been out before breakfast, and when Jensine sat down and loosened her bonnet, the string of pearls caught in her bracelet, and the pearls sprang all over the floor, as if she had burst into a rain of tears. Alexander got down on his hands and knees, and as he picked them up one by one, he placed them in her lap.

She sat in a kind of mild panic. She had broken the one thing in the world that she had been afraid of breaking, what omen did that make to them? "Do you know how many there were?" she asked him.

"Yes," he said from the floor, "Grandpapa gave Grandmamma the string on their golden wedding, with a pearl for each of their fifty years. But afterwards he began to add one every year, on her birthday. There are fifty-two, it is easy to remember, it is the number of cards in a pack."

At last they collected them all, and folded them up in his silk handkerchief.

"Now I cannot put them on till I get to Copenhagen," she said.

At that moment their landlady came in with the coffee; she observed the catastrophe and at once offered to assist them. The shoemaker in the village, she said could do up the pearls for them. Two years ago an English lord and his lady, with a party, had travelled in the mountains, and when the young lady broke her string of pearls, in the same way, he had strung them for her to her perfect satisfaction. He was an honest old man, although very poor, and a cripple. As a young man he had got lost in a snowstorm in the hills, and been found only two days later, and they had had to take off both his feet. Jensine said that she would take her pearls to the shoemaker, and the landlady showed her the way to his house.

She walked down alone, while her husband was strapping their boxes, and found the shoemaker in his little dark workshop. He was a small, thin, old man in a leather apron, with a shy, sly smile in a face harassed by long suffering. She counted out the pearls for him, and gravely confided them into his hands; he looked at them, and promised to have them ready by next midday. After she had settled with him, she kept sitting on a small chair, with her hands in her lap. To say something, she asked him the name of the English lady who had broken her string of pearls, but he did not remember it.

She looked round at the room; it was poor and bare, with a couple of religious pictures nailed on the wall. In a strange way it seemed to her that here she had come home. An honest man, hard-tried by destiny, had passed his long years in this little room; it was a place where people worked, and bore troubles patiently, in anxiety for their daily bread. She was still so near to her school books that she remembered them all, now she began to think of what she

had read about deep-water fish, which have been so
much used to bear the weight of many thousand
fathoms of water, that if they are raised to the sur-
face, they will burst. Was she herself, she wondered,
such a deep-water fish, that felt at home only under
the pressure of existence? Was her father? Had her
grandfather and his people before him, been the
same? What was a deep-water fish to do, she
thought on, if she were married to one of those
salmon which here she had seen springing in the
waterfalls? Or to a flying-fish? She said goodbye to
the old shoemaker, and walked off.

As she was going home she caught sight, on the
path before her, of a small corpulent man in a black
hat and coat, who walked on briskly. She remembered that she had seen him before, she even
believed that he was staying in the same house as
she. There was a seat by the path, from where one
had a magnificent view; the man in black sat down,
and Jensine, whose last day in the mountains it was,
sat down on the other end of the seat. The stranger
lifted his hat a little to her, she had believed him to
be an elderly man, but now saw that he could not be
much over thirty; he had an energetic face, and
clear, penetrating eyes. After a moment he spoke to

her, with a little smile. "I saw you coming out from the shoemaker," he said, "you have not lost your sole in the mountains?"

"No, I took him some pearls," said Jensine.

"You took him pearls?" said the stranger humorously, "that is what I go to collect from him."

She wondered if he were a bit deranged.

"That old man," said he, "has got in his hut, a big store of our old national treasures,—pearls, if you like,—which I happen to be collecting just now. In case you want children's tales, there is not a man in Norway who can give you a better lot than our shoemaker. He once dreamed of becoming a student, and a poet, do you know that?—but he was hard hit by destiny, and had to take to a shoemaker's trade."

After a pause he said: "I have been told that you and your husband come from Denmark, on your wedding trip. That is an unusual thing to do, these mountains are high and dangerous. Which of you two was it who desired to come here? Was it you?"

"Yes," said she.

"Yes," said the stranger, "I thought so, that he might be the bird, which upwards soars and you the breeze, which carries him along. Do you know that quotation? Does it tell you anything?"

"Yes," said she, somewhat bewildered.

"Upwards," said he, and sat back, silent, with his hands upon his walking-stick.

After a little while he went on: "The summit! Who knows? We two are pitying the shoemaker for his bad luck, that he had to give up his dreams of being a poet, of fame and a great name. How do we know but that he has had the best of luck? Greatness, the applause of the masses! Indeed, my young lady, perhaps they are better left alone. Perhaps in common trade they can not reasonably purchase a shoemaker's signboard, and the knowledge of cobbling. One may do well in getting rid of them at cost price. What do you think, Madam?"

"I think that you are right," she said slowly.

He gave her a sharp glance from a pair of ice-blue eyes. "Indeed," said he, "is that your advice, on this fair summer's day? Cobbler, stick to your last. One should do better, you think, in making up pills and draughts for the sick human beings, and cattle, of this world?" He chuckled a little. "It is a very good jest. In a hundred years it will be written in a book: a little lady from Denmark gave him the advice to stick to his last. Unfortunately he did not follow it. Goodbye, Madam, goodbye." With these words he got up, and walked on, she saw his black figure grow smaller amongst the hills. The landlady had come out to ask if she had found the shoemaker. Jensine looked after the stranger. "Who was that gentleman?" she asked.

The woman shaded her eyes with her hand. "Oh, indeed," said she, "he is a learned man, a great man, he is here to collect old stories and songs. He was an apothecary once. But he has had a theatre in Bergen, and written plays for it too. His name is Herr Ibsen."

In the morning, news came up from the landing-place that the boat would be in sooner than expected, and they had to start in haste. The landlady sent her small son to the shoemaker to fetch Jensine's pearls. When the travellers were already seated in the carriage he brought them, wrapped in a leaf from a book, with a tarred string round them. Jensine undid them, and was about to count them, but thought better of it, and instead clasped the string round her throat.

"Ought you not to count them?" Alexander asked.

She gave him a great glance. "No," she said.

She was silent on the drive; his words rang in her ears: "Ought you not to count them?" She sat by his side, a conqueror, now she knew what a conqueror felt like. Alexander and Jensine came back to Copenhagen at a time when most people were out of town, and there were no great social functions. But she had many visits from the wives of his young military friends, and the young people went together to the Tivoli Gardens of Copenhagen in the summer evenings.

Jensine was made much of by all of them. Her house lay by one of the old canals of the town, and looked over to the Thorwaldsen Museum; sometimes she would stand by the window, gaze at the boats and think of Hardanger. During all this time she had not taken off her pearls or counted them. She was sure that there would at least be one pearl missing, she imagined that she felt the weight on her throat different from before. What would it be she thought, which she had sacrificed for her victory over her husband? A year, or two years of their married life, before their golden wedding? This golden wedding seemed a long way off, but still each year was precious, and how was she to part with one of them?

In the last months of this summer, people began to discuss the possibility of war. The Schleswig-Holstein

question had become imminent. A Danish Royal
Proclamation of March had repudiated all German
claims upon Schleswig. Now in July, a German ulti-
matum demanded that it be withdrawn. Jensine was
an ardent patriot and loyal to the King, who had
given the people a free Constitution; the rumours
put her into the highest agitation. She thought the
young officers, Alexander's friends, frivolous in their
light, boastful talk of the country's danger,—if she
wanted to debate it seriously she had to go to her
own people. With her husband she could not talk of
it at all, but in her heart she knew that he was as
convinced of Denmark's invincibility as of his own
immortality. She read the newspapers from begin-
ning to end. One day in the *Berlingske Tidende*, she
came upon the following phrase: "The moment is
grave for the nation. But we have trust in our just
cause, and we are without fear."

It was, perhaps, the words "without fear" which
now made her collect her courage; she sat down in
her chair by the window, took off her pearls and put
them in her lap. She sat for a moment with her
hands folded upon them, as in prayer. Then she
counted them. There were fifty-three pearls on her
string. She could not believe her own eyes, and

counted them over again, but there was no mistake, there were fifty-three pearls and the one in the middle was the biggest.

Jensine sat for a long time in her chair, quite giddy. Her mother, she knew, had believed in the Devil; at this moment the daughter did the same, she would not have been surprised had she heard his laughter from behind the sofa. Had the powers of the Universe, she thought, combined here to make fun of a poor girl? When she could again collect her thoughts, she remembered that before she had been given the necklace, the old goldsmith of her husband's family had repaired the clasp of it, he would therefore know the pearls and might tell her what to believe. But she was so thoroughly scared that she dared not go to him herself, and only a few days later she asked Peter Skov, who came to pay her a visit, to take the string to him.

Peter returned and told her that the goldsmith had put on his spectacles to examine the pearls, and then in amazement had declared that there was one more than when he had last seen them.

"Yes, Alexander gave me that," Jensine interrupted him, blushing deeply at her own lie.

Peter reflected, as the goldsmith had done, that it

was a cheap generosity in a lieutenant to make the heiress he married a rich present. But he repeated to her the old man's words.

"Mr. Alexander," he had declared, "shows himself a rare judge of pearls. I do not hesitate to pronounce this one pearl worth as much as all the others put together." Jensine, terrified but smiling, thanked Peter, but he went away sadly, for he felt as if he had annoyed or frightened her.

She had not been feeling well for some time and when, in September, they had a spell of heavy, sultry weather in Copenhagen, it rendered her pale and sleepless. Her father and her two old aunts were upset about her, and tried to make her come and stay at his Villa on the Strandvej, outside town. But she would not leave her own house or her husband, nor would she, she thought, ever get well, until she had got to the bottom of the mystery of the pearls. After a week, she made up her mind to write to the shoemaker at Odda.

If, as Herr Ibsen had told her, he had been a student and a poet, he would be able to read, and would answer her letter. It seemed to her that in her present situation she had no friend in the world but this crippled old man. She wished that she could go back to his workshop, to the bare walls and the little three-legged chair; she dreamed at night that she was there. He had smiled kindly at her, he knew many children's tales. He might know how to comfort her. Only for a moment she trembled at the idea that he might be dead, and that then she would never know.

With the following weeks the shadow of the war grew deeper. Her father was worrying over the prospects, and about King Frederik's health. Under these new circumstances, the old merchant began to take pride in the fact that he had a daughter married to a soldier; any such connection would have been miles away from him before. He and her old aunts showed Alexander and Jensine great respect.

One day, half against her own will, Jensine asked Alexander straight out if he thought there would be war. Yes, he answered quickly and confidently, there would be war. It could not be avoided.

He went on to whistle a bit of a soldier's song. The sight of her face made him stop. "Are you frightened of it?" he asked. She considered it hopeless and even unseemly to explain to him her feelings about the war.

"Are you frightened for my sake?" he asked her again. She turned her head away.

"To be a hero's widow," he said, "would be just the part for you, my dear." Her eyes filled with tears, as much of anger as of woe.

Alexander came and took her hand. "If I fall," he said, "it will be a consolation to me to remember that I have kissed you as often as you would let me." He did so now once more and added: "Will it be a consolation to you?"

Jensine was an honest girl; when she was questioned she endeavoured to find the truthful answer. Now she thought: Would it be a consolation to me? But she could not, in her heart, find the reply.

With all this Jensine had much to think of, so that she half forgot about the shoemaker, and, when one morning she found his letter on the breakfast table, she for a minute took it to be a mendicant's letter, of which she received many. The next moment she grew very pale. Her husband, opposite her, asked her what was the matter. She gave him no reply, but got up, went into her own small sitting-room, and opened the letter by the fireplace. The characters of it, carefully printed, recalled to her the old man's face as if he had sent her his portrait.

"Dear young Danish Missus," the letter went,

"Yes, I put the pearl on to your necklace. I meant to give you a small surprise. You made such a fuss about your pearls, when you brought them to me, as if you were afraid that I should steal one of them from you. Old people, as well as young, must have a little fun at times. If I have frightened you, I beg that you will forgive me all the same. This pearl I got two years ago, when I strung the English lady's necklace, I forgot to put the one in, and only found it afterwards. It has been with me for two years, but I have no use for it, it is better that it should be with a young lady. I remember that you sat in my chair, quite young and pretty. I wish you good luck, and that something pleasant may happen to you upon the very same day as you get this letter. And may you wear the pearl long, with a humble heart, a firm trust in the Lord God, and a friendly thought of me, who am old, here up at Odda. Goodbye.

Your friend, Peiter Viken."

Jensine had been reading the letter with her elbows on the mantelpiece, to steady herself. As she looked up, she met the grave eyes of her own image in the looking-glass above it. They were severe, they might be saying: "You are really a thief, or if not that, a receiver of stolen goods, and no better than a thief."

She stood for a long time, nailed to the spot. At last she thought: "It is all over. Now I know that I shall never conquer these people, who know neither care nor fear. It is as in the Bible: I shall bruise their heel, but they shall bruise my head. And Alexander, as far as he is concerned, ought to have married the English lady."

To her own deep surprise, she found that she did not mind. Alexander, himself, had become a very small figure in the background of her life, what he did or thought mattered not in the least. That she herself had been made a fool of did not matter. "In a hundred years," she thought, "it will all be one."

What mattered then? She tried to think of the war, but found that the war did not matter either. She felt a strange giddiness, as if the room was sinking away round her, but not unpleasantly. "Was there," she thought, "nothing left remarkable under the visiting moon?" At the word of the visiting moon, the eyes of the image in the looking-glass opened wide, the two young women stared at one another intensely. Something, she decided, was of great importance, which had come into the world now, and in a hundred years would still remain. The pearls. In a hundred years, she saw, a young man would hand them over to his wife and tell the young woman her own story about them, just as Alexander had given them to her and had told her of his grandmother.

The thought of these two young people, in a hundred years' time, moved her to such tenderness that her eyes filled with tears and made her happy, as if they had been old friends of hers, whom she had found again.

"Not cry quarter?" she thought, "Why not? Yes, I shall cry as loud as I can. I cannot, now, remember the reason why I would not cry."

The very small figure of Alexander, by the window in the other room, said to her: "Here is the eldest of your Aunts coming down the street with a big bouquet."

Slowly, slowly, Jensine took her eyes off the looking-glass, and came back to the world of the present. She went to the window. "Yes," she said, "they are from Bella Vista," which was the name of her father's villa.

Each from their window, the husband and wife, looked down into the street.